MW00423517

30 Days to Shine

Y'all Are Crazy Devotional Series

Y'all Are Crazy Publishing LLC
Written by: Ashley Schubert
Edited by: Brittanie Ebrite
Cover Design by: Hilarie Salamone

INTRODUCTION

Most of this devotional was written on my back porch looking over the pond with the fountain sounding softly in the background. It's pretty and sunny and the grass is green. It's morning, is quiet and the kids are still asleep. I have a few minutes before all the craziness begins. Soon, the kids will wake up and our chaotic day will begin. My days consist of snacks and sippy cups, cleaning up messes and trying to entertain my kids during the summer days. It also consists of working and building a business simultaneously. I'm truly raising a business and babies (just like I wrote about in my first book). My passion is helping women flourish. I feel led to share my stories and my struggles so that other women can feel inspired and thrive. I pray that my experiences, thoughts and my life can stand out in a way that others see Jesus in me. That's my overall goal. I pray this devotional encourages you and gives you 30 days to SHINE!

DAY 1: LISTENING

They say "You gotta see it to believe it". God says "You gotta believe it to see it". I decide what I sow. He's the God of the outcome. I heard this message from Pastor Steven Furtick of Elevation Church and it jumped out at me! It totally goes against society's views of faith and seeing. God has a different way for us. He wants us to plant the seeds, put the work in and prepare. Only He can bring the rain.

Have you ever seen the movie "Facing the Giants"? It's an amazing faith-based movie by the Kendrick Brothers. It's about a struggling high school football coach who has trouble trusting God. When he finally decides to do so and goes all in, he receives a message from an older, wiser friend. "God will bring the rain when He's ready. You have got to prepare your fields." And that's just what he does! He starts training his players, not only on skill set of the game, but on integrity on and off the field. He turns his life around, and in turn, the football season goes from a losing one to winning a state championship. On the last play of the game, the coach knows it's his chance to prepare for rain and let God bring it. The other coaches think he's crazy but he says these three powerful words when asked what in the world he is doing. "I'm preparing for rain".

God wants to bless you- in your life, your family, your business. But he needs you to do the work, plant the seeds, have faith. He needs you to take the steps. Prepare for rain. He's the God of the outcome.

Remember this: whoever sows sparingly, will also reap sparingly, and whoever sows generously will also reap generously.
2 Corinthians 9:6

How are you preparing for God's blessings today?

DAY 2: YOU'RE NOT READY YET

My kids were swimming at a pool party this summer. They aren't quite ready to be skilled swimmers yet but they think they can! The older two kept begging me to take off their life jackets and I kept on saying "No" over and over again, "You're not ready", "the water will go over your head", "you don't have the right skills yet". And then I realized, my kids don't know what it feels like to sink, to go underwater and be afraid. I have always been their protector, their safety net. I knew that they needed lessons, time and practice before they would be ready to take off those life jackets. They only knew that it looked fun and they had no concept of fear. I made a bold "mom-move". I said "go take off your life jackets and get in. Remember, stay calm and swim to the edge if you get scared". They jumped in the shallow end with smiles on their faces. They began walking into the deep end, and then - the fear set in! My son got a terrified look on his face and he began doggy paddling as hard as he could, working hard to keep his head above the water. I let him struggle a bit. He never went under but his head bobbed up and down as he struggled to get to the edge. I extended my arm out and pulled him over. He took a breath of relief. I looked him in the eye and said, "I want you to learn how to swim but until you do, you must wear your life jacket to help you float so you can be safe and have fun in the pool." He shook his head in agreement and I saw relief flash across his face. I was certain that he had learned his lesson.

Isn't it that way with God sometimes? When we want our way and we say "Now, God! Why not now?" God says "You're not ready yet. I am developing your character and you are still growing. You need more time." And then when we keep pushing and want it on our own timing, God says "Go ahead and try it." We do it on our own and fail. We scurry, we become overwhelmed, we realize that we did need more time. We were not ready yet and needed to be still and wait for the Lord. Sometimes, God lets us learn lessons the hard way, just as I did with my son. It doesn't mean He doesn't love us. Quite the contrary, He loves us so much that He allows us to fail, to learn and to realize that we need Him and His direction will never lead us astray.

But they who wait for the Lord shall renew
their strength; they shall mount up with
wings like eagles; they shall run and not be
weary; they shall walk and not faint.
Isaiah 40:31

What are you rushing to do when God is saying "You're Not Ready Yet"?

DAY 3: CALLING

We can sometimes question our calling. Maybe we heard God wrong or we got mixed up on what path to take. Sometimes we want to exchange our gifts with someone else.

I felt called to lead a small group at my church one year. I was super busy at work and at home with the kids, of course. But I knew God was asking me to step out in faith. So I said yes. It was a very success-ful venture with a great group of women attending. There was growth and stories of victory each week.

And then, there came the negative person who threw me off course. She told one of our pastors that I was only leading the group for personal gain. And that I didn't care about the women or the church as a whole. When I was approached about this, I was angry, distraught, and shocked. I handled the situ-ation professionally on the outside. On the inside, I questioned everything. I felt like my integrity had been called into check. I talked to my husband that evening with tears in my eyes. He listened to my sobs and was attentive to my breaking self-esteem.

"Maybe God didn't call me to lead?"

"Maybe everyone feels this way about me?"
"I wish I could give this gift of leadership and influence back." I said that evening.

And then, through prayer, God showed me that He gave me my gifts and abilities for a reason. They were to be used and not wasted. He reminded me that in this world we would have trouble but He had overcome the world.

For God is working in you, giving you the desire and the power to do what pleases Him.
Philippians 2:13

What is God calling you to use your gifts for right now?

DAY 4: NOT RIGHT NOW

I have a list of "crazy goals" I hope to achieve in my life. Some of these are so big that I would be afraid to show anyone. People and my family would say "You can't do that right now. Why would you want that? Aren't you content with this? Fill in the blank." While I know some of my dreams might seem scary, big, or just unreachable, I also know there is a God who put these dreams in my heart when He created me. One in particular has plagued me and I cannot let it go even over time. While I still feel compelled toward it, I have a place that God is whispering "Not right now". Not "never", just not this minute. As an Enneagram 3, I struggle with this. The Enneagram is a personality type test and every test I take of this sort lands on one word for me "achiever".

Achievers get things done.

Achievers want things and do whatever it takes to get them.

Achievers want a timeline and we want everything to happen now or at the latest tomorrow.

I have had to let myself rest in knowing that God has it all figured out and that He has the ultimate power. His plans for me are good, even in the "not right now". I can trust that His timing is perfect and I can rest today in knowing that His plans are to prosper me.

For I know the plans I have for you, declares the Lord, plans to prosper you and not to harm you, plans to give you hope and a future.
Jeremiah 29:11

What are your big goals that may not happen right now?

DAY 5: THE DIFFERENCE IN DOORS

I have a hard time sitting still. Like literally, I can't sit down for too long or I start feeling tired of sitting around and waiting and I need a change. I struggle with sitting down during the day to read or just rest. It's the "achiever" side of me. It's also a thorn in my side sometimes. It's hard to be content because I'm always reaching for more. Often, I come to a door and I think "Is this God opening a door or am I forcing it open?'

That's a tough question but I believe it all comes down to having "peace" and letting the Holy Spirit speak. I pray to feel peace in my next right move and peace to know it's okay to move forward. I am very risk averse. Risks do not bother us, my husband and I, which is awesome yet also crazy. I like to pray for peace, discernment and wisdom before making decisions. God will not speak audibly like He did in the Biblical days. But He will give us a "STOP" feeling in our hearts OR a peace feeling that says "GO". When God says GO, be prepared to go forward in His peace.

It won't always be easy to go forward. Many times it won't make sense. Some people will even discourage you. But, don't worry or fear. If God puts a dream in your heart and He wants to open a door, rest assured, it will open. You will just need to do your part and knock. Knock, knock, knock. God will open the door.

And the peace of God, which transcends all understanding, will guard your hearts and minds in Christ Jesus.
Philippians 4:7

Are you being called to "go" or to "stop" right now?

DAY 6: STARTING NEW CLUBS

I was always the girl starting clubs in school. Even back in my elementary years I was starting little clubs with my friends - including a lemonade stand club, Rugrats and "The Babysitters Club" (if you grew up in the 1990s you will remember that book and tv series). I was always all-inclusive, if you wanted to join, come on in! It was always the "cool kids" who stayed away, laughed at the kids in my "clubs" and teased us as we played. I never cared.

I gave everyone in the club a role and delegated tasks. It's funny to think back on that now because does a lemonade stand club really need a list of officers? I even designed our brand and picked out colors. I was probably in 3rd grade at this point. I was never afraid to start something or recruit and build a board around it.

It's ironic to see how my life has played out. I am now in a real business as an adult, where I recruit, build my brand and tune out the nay-sayers and negativity. All the time, God was preparing me for my future. He used my natural skills as a child and turned them into my best skills as an adult. He had a plan all along and as always, it was better than mine.

Whatever you do, work heartily, as for the Lord and not for men, knowing that from the Lord you will receive the inheritance as your reward.
Colossians 3:23-24

What are your natural skills and talents God gave you, even as a child?

DAY 7: FLYING

I remember the first time I flew in an airplane. I was sixteen years old and I had recently won a trip to Washington D.C. I had been selected amongst a group of high school students around the country by winning an essay and speech contest. My family had always vacationed by car and I had never had the need to fly. In this case, I was nervous and my tummy felt this. We took off and had a smooth flight but upon landing I began feeling nauseous. I grabbed the trash bag in the seat back in front of me and I threw up right there. Surrounded by other high school juniors, sitting next to a cute boy I had just met, I lost it all.

Even though that time was highly embarrassing and forever etched in my memory, I never stopped flying. Since then, I have flown dozens of times to places all over. I have been to Paris, Mexico, Hawaii and all over the U.S. I have seen Glacier National Park and Yosemite, San Diego, Florida and many, many more beautiful places. I did continue to throw up upon landing for several years (I still don't know what that was about) and I still dislike flying. But every time I face my fear, take the chance of throwing up in front of everyone (Ha Ha!) and hop on the plane. If I would have stopped flying because I let my fear overcome me, I would have missed out on seeing some amazing sights and places! Sometimes, our uncomfortable places are worth it.

Sometimes, I still throw up when I fly. And it's still embarrassing. It's always upon landing and I don't know why. It doesn't stop me from traveling because the embarrassment and uncomfortable 5 minutes are overshadowed by the experiences that lie ahead!

In the same way, let your light shine before others, so that they may see your good works and give glory to your Father who is in heaven.
Matthew 5:16

What do you love to do but it makes you uncomfortable? Is it worth the discomfort to get the reward?

DAY 8: I'M NOT GOOD AT RELAXING

I'm such a doer, a get it done person and a "no excuses" woman, that it's really hard for me to relax. Even taking an hour out of my day to have some self-care leaves me feeling behind and unworthy.

I had a massage today and I enjoyed every minute of it. It was relaxing and much needed. But even as it was in session, I kept thinking about my to-do list and all I needed to accomplish. After it was over, I was already worrying about if I took too much time away from my kids or from my business. Was I selfish? Did I really deserve it? Should I really be taking time for myself when I have four kids and a business to run? Yes, I have to remind myself. It's okay to have margin, room to breathe and spaces of rest. It's okay not to have a plan and to take care of myself instead of everyone else for an hour.

Maybe I can get better at this someday. Right now, I

will just enjoy the time I am getting and make the most of the little relaxing moments.

For me, I have learned that this means: putting my feet up and watching Netflix with my husband at the end of the day, taking a hot shower before bed each night (or sitting in the hot tub if I'm lucky), or taking a couple hours to get a massage or a pedicure. Maybe it's reading a book for an hour on a Sunday afternoon with a hot cup of tea. These are all simple ideas but are so difficult when your mind is always looking at your to-do list. Lord, help me get better about refreshment.

Come to me, all who labor and are heavy laden, and I will give you rest. Matthew 11:28

When are your times of rest and refreshment? Do you ever feel guilty about these?

DAY 9: FAITH IS SPELLED R-I-S-K

We have never been conventional in the way we buy and sell houses. Being a realtor, I know the right ways to stage a home and can keep a close eye on market trends. I can see when homes comparable to ours are selling really well and for top dollar. Our first, second, and third homes were purchased from sellers who were desperately trying to get out of their mortgages. We always found a way to make them a good enough offer to accept while leaving enough for us to have instant equity.

I sold our second home without putting it on the market, simply through word of mouth and directly reaching out to a prospective buyer. Our third home was a little bit more of a risk since we loved it. It worked well for our family's needs and was in a desirable location. But, we saw the equity potential in the market and wanted something our family could grow into. God was shaping our hearts for our next season.

During the uneasiness, doubt about the future and

the fear of failure; I remembered that God had a plan. My past experiences reminded me that faith is spelled "RISK".

"Truly I tell you, if you have faith as small as a mustard seed, you can say to this mountain, 'move from here to there' and it will move. Nothing will be impossible for you." Matthew 17:20

Is there a risk you need to take today?

DAY 10: START BEFORE YOU ARE READY

If I had to summarize my successes in life into one piece of advice, it would likely be: "start before you are ready."

We started our real estate brokerage in May 2019 after only discussing the idea for less than two months. Those two months were filled with planning and discussion but nothing qualified my partner and I to open a real estate brokerage. We were great agents in our respect, yes. But we had never really thought about what it took to start a brokerage and we did a little research before signing up and literally "posting a sign on the door".

If we had waited for a less crazy season, would it have been easier? Yes.
If we had gotten all our policies and procedures ironed out to a fine science, would we have been more prepared? Yes.

If we had waited until our kids grew up and we had more time, would it have been safer? Yes.

Do I regret it? No.
Have I learned a ton in a short time? Yes.
Would I do it again? Yes.

You see, when we start before we are ready, we can learn, mature and grow in the process! This is the case when having and raising a family, making a move or starting a business! Here is the key: you'll never be ready. Just start.

I've decided that there's nothing better to do than go ahead and have a good time and get the most we can out of life. That's it - eat, drink and make the most of your job. It's God's gift.
Ecclesiastes 3:12-13

Are you ready to make a bold move but worried about the timing?

DAY 11: AS FOR ME AND MY HOUSE

We will serve the Lord. Joshua 24:15

We have a sign on our back patio with this scripture. It's displayed proudly, sitting higher than anything else. There is a reason why I love this verse so much, even though it is used so often.

Each day we must make the choice to turn against the world, culture and the norm. We take a stand and say- " As for me and my house."

Anytime a friend or family member looks down on us, teases us, or put us down to make themselves feel better, we can smile and proclaim - "As for me and my house."

Whenever Satan tries to throw a wrench in our plans and mess up what we want to accomplish, we can rebuke him and say - "As for me and my house."

There are many ways to use this verse on a daily

basis and it is applicable in many areas of our lives. It can give us confidence that no matter what our family WILL serve the Lord.

But as for me and my house, we will serve the Lord.
Joshua 24:15

What is true for you and your house today?

DAY 12: HOBBIES

I started playing golf at 32 years old. I grew up as a serious athlete, always with a basketball or a softball bat in my hands. I loved the adrenaline and the challenge that sports provided. I loved the pressure and learned so many life lessons. Even in college, I continued to play weekly and probably took it more seriously than I should have, even though I always had fun.

When I started having babies, my free time diminished and having a hobby became non-existent. The only time I had away from my kids is when I was working. My passion became my work and while that was a good thing for my business, it also put me on the road to burnout.

I realized this was happening and decided I needed an outlet to help me feel alive and something for myself, besides work. I took up golf and felt myself enjoying it so much. My husband and I could play together. We could be outdoors and we could just have fun! Having a fun hobby made a difference in my overall happiness and it also made me enjoy my time with my kids more! Plus, it made me want to go to work and renewed that passion as well!

From the fruit of his mouth a man is satisfied with good, and the work of a man's hand comes back to him. Proverbs 12:14

What is a hobby you could enjoy? Maybe it's crafting, reading, or going to the gym. Don't feel guilty to take a little time for yourself.

DAY 13: COUNTER-CULTURAL

If we only live as the "norm", we can never experience God's power to work in the impossible.

Being a realtor, I understand the business of buying and selling houses. I know home values, current market trends and the right way to stage a home. Because of that I am able to put our house up for sale in a moment's notice. We have sold two homes like this, when we really didn't know where we were going to move next. We just knew God was calling us elsewhere. We knew that He would make a way when there seems to be no way and we would find the next perfect place. In turn, our home would provide the perfect home for the next family.

You see, culture tells us to avoid risk. Only do what you can do in front of you and never just trust God. But, my friend, the Bible teaches us the opposite. The Bible is all about faith without seeing. I believe

God calls us to be "lion chasers". If you haven't read Mark Batterson's "In a Pit With a Lion On a Snowy Day', I highly encourage it. That book gave me the Biblical name for our fourth-born "Benaiah".

When we chase instead of just letting life happen, God can use His power and show us His glory. We only need to stop being afraid to step out in faithfulness. I'm not saying we make dumb choices. We must pray about things, calculate, discuss - but then, when God calls us to say yes, we must GO.

Be strong and courageous. Do not be frightened, and do not be dismayed, for the Lord your God is with you wherever you go. Joshua 1:9

What do you need to CHASE?

DAY 14: NEXT PHASE, PLEASE

One thing I have learned about being a mom and raising kids is this: they grow up. Sometimes it feels slow and the days feel long. Sometimes it seems like they will never get out of up-all-night newborn days, the terrible twos or the long summer days where you want to pull your hair out. But those days too, they pass. The kids move from one phase to the next. We look up and they are onto the next thing. I feel like each phase has its own challenges. The truth is, we learn as much about being a parent as they do being a kid. Sometimes I feel like I get one thing figured out, like breastfeeding and baby wearing, and I have to learn potty training and sight word recognition. I want to tell my kids "Hey guys, Momma is learning and figuring this out right along with ya!"

God doesn't expect us to have it all figured out. But he does want us to grow and fully enjoy the days we have instead of spending them overwhelmed and stressed. We can choose to spend them giving ourselves some grace and let our kids live fully in the moment before they move from this phase to the next.

My husband wears a bracelet that we got a parenting conference at church. It says "It's just a phase, don't miss it". He says it reminds him to be present in the moment and to enjoy the moments, the days and the phases.

Don't you see that children are God's best gift? The fruit of the womb his generous legacy? Like a warrior's fistful of arrows are the children of a vigorous youth. Oh, how blessed are you parents, with your quivers full of children! Your enemies don't stand a chance against you; you'll sweep them right off your doorstep.
Psalm 127:3-5

What phase are you in? What can you enjoy in this phase?

DAY 15: THE GREY AREAS

I have been reading Proverbs a lot lately. It's filled with scripture about wisdom. It's also filled with verses about avoiding "evil" and "wrongdoing". When I hear these words I instantly think "Well, of course I will avoid evil." The tricky thing about life is that most of our decisions aren't black and white. Most choices lie in the grey area.

Evil or no evil? I'll choose no evil, thanks.

But what about a common occurence of choosing whether or not to gossip with a friend?
Or hand back extra change we receive at the checkout line?
Or what about taking an item back in to pay for it when we accidentally leave it at the bottom of our shopping basket?

These choices come without a black and white solution, but rather with a choice that lies in grey areas. It's not really wrong is it? But is it exceptional? Is it God's way? If you were to ask yourself

"WWJD", like our bracelets back in the 90s said, what conclusion would we draw?

You see, life is filled with hard choices. Most aren't cut and dry, easy-peasy, no brainers.

Most require us to search inside our hearts and our Bibles and let the Holy Spirit determine our outcomes.

Finally, brothers, whatever is true, whatever is honorable, whatever is just, whatever is pure, whatever is lovely, whatever is commendable, if there is any excellence, if there is anything worthy of praise, think about these things. Philippians 4:8

What "grey" areas have you struggled with in the past?

DAY 16: HONOR THE LORD WITH YOUR RICHES

I know, "riches" sound like you must be a queen or live in a kingdom or have celebrity status.

But riches simply mean the best you have.

If you have a salary job and are on a strict budget, your best maybe a set amount or maybe above and beyond that.

God wants us to honor Him with our riches. That means through tithes and offerings. It also means with our resources.

Having a nice home has always been important for us. We have a large family so we need the space. But we also love hosting at our place - cookouts, birthday parties, we even held my sister in law's wedding on our front porch. We understand that God gave us everything we own. Therefore, we want to honor Him by opening up our house to others.

Another way we can use our resources is through our talents. Maybe that's serving in childcare at church (God bless the childcare workers!). Maybe it's singing, cooking, or planning. You can use your skills and talents to serve God.

So bring your "riches", whether in money or your resources or talents to bring glory to God.

Honor the Lord with your wealth and with the first fruits of all your produce; then your barns will be filled with plenty, and your vats will be bursting with wine. Proverbs 3:9-10

What "riches" do you need to honor God with this year?

DAY 17: GOD WILL ALWAYS GIVE US MORE THAN WE CAN HANDLE

It's been said "God will never give you more than you can handle." Yes, <u>He will</u>! That's kind of the point. God will always give us more than we can handle so we will trust in Him, let Him work through us, and show His glory.

I have noticed that anytime we "give it to God" he will give us more than we can handle. It's overwhelming at times and the hard times make us question ourselves, but they should never make us doubt God.

When you feel like you have more than you can handle, REJOICE! You are right where God wants you to be. Now, remember to trust in Him and He will make your paths straight.

Rejoice when you face trials of many kinds. Trials

build character and wisdom and you will be more thankful for the trials than the successes. The trials teach us more than we could ever learn by staying safe and secure. Trials are God's way of saying "I got you, now learn from this". God will always give you more than you can handle. Now rely on Him and learn what he is trying to teach you.

Trust in the Lord with all your heart, and do not lean on your own understanding. In all your ways acknowledge Him, and He will make straight your paths.
Proverbs 3:5-6

What can you rejoice about, even though it feels like a trial?

DAY 18: REFRESHMENT

When you pour into others all the time, whether as a church volunteer, friend or even as a mom, you would think you would feel depleted.

But, I find that as I bless others and speak life into them. I feel more refreshed.

This makes sense because it is a promise in God's word. It's true that we receive when we fully give. When we tithe, our own finances thrive. When we are generous with our time, we end up with more quality. When we "give" God our families, business and overall lives and trust Him to take control, we feel relief.

So, be generous, not just monetarily but with your time, with your kind words and encouragement. Refresh others and pour yourself out. God promises He will use His refreshing to fill you back up. And when He does, it will be with joy overflowing.

My cup has overflowed - as a child, I sang in church

often. I sang one song called - "Drinking from my saucer" and the words of that song are so powerful.

The generous will prosper. Those who refresh others will be refreshed. Proverbs 11:25

In what way do you need to be generous?

DAY 19: GUILT

Do you know any mom who doesn't struggle with guilt? I sure don't. Every mom I know feels guilty about something - her kid's childcare, her cooking, quality time, working, you name it. We women always seem to feel guilty about something. And guilt is crippling - it does nothing but knock us down, bring down our spirit, and leave us feeling discouraged. Satan knows he can attack us best when our spirits and self-worth are down and we feel we don't measure up.

I say it's time we stand up and say "no more"! This is a daily battle where we must rebuke the lies of the enemy and move forward in faith, knowing that our worth is found in who God says we are. Not in who other people say we are. When our perspective changes, our view changes. Our guilt can vanish if we rebuke it and replace it with God's truth daily.

I will not feel guilty about being a mom and spending time with my kids.
I will not feel guilty about working and enjoying it.
I will not feel guilty about working out and making sure I'm healthy.

I will not feel guilty about resting. I need refreshment. (Still working on this one!)

> *Let the peace of Christ rule in your hearts,*
> *since as members of one body you were*
> *called to peace. And be thankful.*
> *Colossians 3:15*

> *In what area do you need to remind yourself*
> *of letting go of the guilt? Write it down.*

DAY 20: PERSEVERANCE

If you haven't started a new thing as an adult, it's so much harder than when you were a kid. Past comforts must be corrected, like my softball swing. I spent most of my life swinging a softball bat, which is the complete opposite of swinging a golf club. So, I had to correct my swing, play often enough to improve, listen to advise, and get help from others who played often.

Being an athlete and competitor, there were times when I just wanted to throw in the towel and be done with it. Surely there was a better way to spend my time where I didn't just feel like a failure. But then, one of my friends told me "golf has a two year learning curve". That shifted my perspective.

I wasn't supposed to step in and be good right away. I wasn't supposed to be able to hit it like a pro the first summer I played. The key was sticking with it, practice and perseverance. If I do those things, my unnatural ability will start to become more natural as I train my body to do something new.

*I press on toward the goal for the prize of the
upward call of God in Christ Jesus.
Philippians 3:14*

*What is not natural for you but you want
it to become more natural?*

DAY 21: THE MAGIC OF MARGIN

I have had to make the decision to step away from a few things lately. I had gotten myself into a place of busy-ness with no room for margin. I had packed my schedule so tight that I had no room for rest, restoration or grace. It was all about getting things done, checking things off my schedule and pleasing everyone involved. And then it hit me. I was exhausted.

I prayed about it and made the decision to eliminate a few time commitments that I needed to let go of this season. It was hard because I felt like I was letting people down and I was scared that I would lose friends, lose my busy-ness that I had grown so accustomed to. But it was necessary.

By making that decision, I cut down on my to-do list and opened up my mind for creativity and gave my body room for restoration. It was needed.

In different seasons, we must examine what is working for our family, ourself and our lifestyle. We must choose to cut out and to add. We must choose to say "no" to things and "yes" to others at the right time. Everything has a season.

> *For everything there is a season, and a time*
> *for every matter under heaven.*
> *Ecclesiastes 3:1*

Do you have room for margin in your life?

DAY 22: JESUS COULDN'T KEEP EVERYONE HAPPY

Some days, I base my mood on others feelings or reactions. Because someone may have said hurtful words to me yesterday or left a snarky comment on my Facebook page, it can wreck my day if I let it. I am a people pleaser by nature so I want people to know, like and trust me. When I feel like someone doesn't, I feel defeated. But that isn't what God wants for us. He doesn't want us to start our day off in defeat.

We cannot control others thoughts or actions but we can control our own. We can keep ourselves positive and our minds right. We can stay upbeat and enthusiastic! We can remember that what God says about us has the final authority.

When we feel put down, discouraged or like we

don't measure up, we can remember that we are called to live lives that please God, not to live lives that keep others happy. Even Jesus couldn't keep everyone happy. There was always a pharisee or king upset with Him. If Jesus couldn't keep everyone happy, why on Earth would we think we can?

Start your day with prayer, praise and confidence!

Let the words of my mouth and the meditation of my heart be acceptable in your sight, oh Lord, my rock and my redeemer.
Psalms 19:14

What do you need to let go of today that you are only doing to please others?

DAY 23: HAPPY FOR NOW

What does it take to bring happiness? A good day without frustration or trouble? A new car? A new job? Maybe, for a while but happiness is so fleeting. That new car, job and all the things that can make us happy, they become old news and our happiness fades like the morning dew.

Joy is different and can only be found in God's people, in those who love Him and place their hope in Him. It's unending, undying, and it's real.

On days when I am feeling blue, even for no reason, I remember God is with me. He is the source of my joy, not earthly things. It's ALL about Him, not me or this world.

Temporary happiness can never replace joy. Happiness is for now, joy is for always.

"I've got the joy, joy, joy, joy down in my heart". I played that song as a child.

Count it all joy, my brothers, when you meet

trials of various kinds, for you know that the testing of your faith produces steadfastness.
James 1:2-3

What brings you joy? Write down five things and focus on doing them more!

DAY 24:
DEDICATED TIME
TOGETHER

My husband and I have four kids and have been married ten years at this point. Our time alone is limited, as we are usually surrounded by loud children, the joy of our lives. We discovered that we missed spending time together and needed time to connect with each other on a regular basis. For a while, that meant having a sitter and going on a date once a month. That was refreshing and felt good for a while. Once we started golfing together, we decided we could use that time as a date. Our club had a good childcare program, so each Tuesday we would drop the kids off, play a few holes of golf and then have dinner together. It was so refreshing and brought us closer together. We called it "Tuesday Tee Time".

Relationships thrive when we spend time together - whether with our spouses, kids, or with GOD!

My kids love it when I spend one-on-one time with them. That's hard to do when you have a few! But, it's important to be intentional and spend individual time with them to learn about them and show your love. Sometimes, for us, it's a trip to Braum's to get ice cream or a shopping spree at Dollar Tree (Pro Mom Tip: Take your kids to Dollar Tree and tell them they can get anything in the store they want! They will think they won the lottery!) It doesn't matter what you do. They just want to spend time with you.

Every good and perfect gift is from above, coming down from the Father of the heavenly lights, who does not change like the shifting shadows.
James 1:17

Who do you need to have dedicated time with regularly? How can you plan to do that?

DAY 25: THE GRASS IS GREENER

In the heat of a summer morning, I can look out and see the green grass before me. If you can get out before 10 a.m. it's an enjoyable time to be outside. After that, it can be so hot in July and August in Oklahoma. Therefore, we must take advantage of the mornings and evenings in the summertime. You'll often hear people say "I cannot wait for Fall.", "Winter can't come soon enough.", "I'm so tired of this heat." I can't blame them. The extreme heat is miserable and 99 degree days are rough and even dangerous. When I feel this way, I try to remind myself that Winter will be here soon enough and then we will be wishing for summer. We will miss the sunshine and long days, the green grass and the cool evening breeze.

It's the same way in life. We rush the days, months, and seasons, just waiting for the next big thing. Once we get there, we miss the days before and realize we took them for granted.

Enjoy the days because the grass isn't always greener. Just like the weather, our days and life circumstances change, day by day. We must enjoy the good times, we must grow in the hard times, we must rely on God in the sad times and we must take not take any day for granted. Use each day to serve Him and let Him work through you.

In the morning, Lord, you hear my voice; in the morning
I lay my requests before you and wait expectantly.
Psalms 5:3

What season are you in right now
that you just need to enjoy?

DAY 26: MAKING FRIENDS IS HARD

Wow…I used to have so many friends. In high school and college, I was never lacking in the friends department. Now I look around and I'm like "Where are my friends?"

As women and moms, we give and pour out of ourselves. Whether it be in our careers, our homes, raising our children, at our church, to our husbands, and the list goes on. We don't realize until the time comes, that we have lost friendships and those are things that used to matter so much. Our high school friends went different ways after graduation. Same with our college buddies, as each got married, started careers and moved away. We forgot to make new ones somehow along the way and realize how nice it would be to have women to talk to and hang out with. Sometimes, we need to join groups, sometimes we need to start the group.

We can either wait to be invited or we can create friendships. We can initiate the relationships and get them started. It's uncomfortable but community is necessary. Community is worthwhile.

We will make friends, we will lose friends. Some people are friends for a season, some are friends for a lifetime. It's okay if it's just for a season. Give yourself freedom in that. Just make sure you are surrounding yourself with friends who you can pour into and around those who can pour into you!

And day by day, attending the temple together and breaking bread in their homes, they received their food with glad and generous hearts.
Acts 2:46

How can you form new relationships in your life?

DAY 27: BRAVE AND KIND

If I could choose two words for my kids that could show them the keys to happiness and a fulfilled life, it would be these two - Brave and Kind. Brave enough to be bold and take risks to go after what they want. Kind enough to be a friend, treat others well and let God's light shine.

Bravery comes from repetition and by seeing and doing. It takes practice in order to show my kids what it's like to be brave, to pursue your dreams and to take the risks worth taking.

Kindness comes from the heart. I want to model this virtue for my children in the way I treat others and live daily life. Kids pick up on all the little ways they see us behave and the things we say. Kindness, that simple term, should be a way of living.

I want to model these two words from them. I want to show them how to live in this way. I want them to learn from me but I know I cannot do this perfectly. They have to learn how to be brave and kind on their own, through their own experiences. May my children always be brave and kind - just as I always strive to be brave and kind.

Be strong and courageous. Do not be frightened, and do not be dismayed, for the Lord your God is with you wherever you go.
Joshua 1:9

What two words do you want others to say about you?

DAY 28: THE GREY

Have you ever been faced with choice with no clear path? Two decisions and only one way to go. Of course you have. In fact we all have. We have all been given tough choices to make when it comes down to it, we must make the right choice. The right choice can determine our future outcomes. That's where we start getting afraid and paralyzed.

Knowing which path to take is truly the hardest part of all. The paths aren't always clear and straight. The right path isn't always easy to choose. Life isn't black and white. There are many grey areas. When you're at a crossroads, be prepared to be okay with the grey. Move forward in the grey. The worst choice you can make is no choice at all.

Through prayer and petition, present your requests to God. He will make your paths straight and will answer your prayers. If you cannot make a choice that seems so grey, when you want a black-and-white answer, prayerfully and confidently move forward in the grey.

Do not be anxious about anything, but in every situation, by prayer and petition, with

thanksgiving, present your requests to God.
Philippians 4:6

What choice are you trying to make but it's not black and white? How can you move forward in the grey?

DAY 29: BUILDING A BRAND

One of the most important parts of starting a business is creating a brand, a culture if you will. You must determine what you want to be known for.

In our social media driven world, creating a "brand" for yourself is more important than ever. You must decide what you want to be known for.

We all know people who are always super dramatic, very negative, or maybe even those who are upbeat and funny. On Facebook, that's the way we see these people.

The funny thing is, they have created how they want to be known and perceived. They have built their own brand, maybe without even realizing it.

You can choose the image you want, you can choose the person you want to be, and you can live the life you want to live. The choice is yours. Start building your "brand", in business and in life.

Do not be conformed to this world, but be

transformed by the renewal of your mind, that by testing you may discern what is the will of God, what is good and acceptable and perfect.
Romans 12:2

What is your personal brand? Do people know that about you?

DAY 30: SWEET SPOT

Living in a way that makes us feel happy and whole is comforting.

Think back to what makes you feel warm and cozy: drinking a warm cup of coffee, reading a book on a rainy day, or baking pumpkin bread on a Saturday morning. That's your sweet spot. Now, what's your sweet spot in life?

Are you really good at math, writing, computers, communication? What comes naturally to you? Now use that thing and make it into something you can do, either monetarily or charity.

Using our God given strengths for His purpose and glory are the best way to reach people.

When we play to our strengths, it should feel like we are in our "sweet spot". It should feel effortless, warm and cozy.

Use your sweet spot and make an impact!

So we, though many, are one body in Christ, and

individually members one of another. Having gifts that differ according to the grace given to us, let us use them.
Romans 12:5-6

What's your "sweet spot", even if you have never thought about it before?

ASHLEY'S READING RECOMMEN- DATION

Obviously, I love to write. I also love to read. I read fiction every night for enjoyment. I like Christian fiction and my favorite authors are Karen Kingsbury and Colleen Coble. They are both great authors and their books are easy to read. Plus they are filled with suspense. They leave you feeling closer to God and the characters are entertaining.

I also like reading non-fiction and learning how to better myself and my business. For me, reading these books requires a highlighter and a notebook because I want to remember everything I'm reading. It's a great way to learn and grow.

Mixing it up with fiction and non-fiction helps me not take myself too seriously and creates a good rhythm in my life.

Reading the Bible is obviously the ideal choice for reading and it can speak to you differently every time you read it!

Reading is good for your mind and your spirit. It can impact you in so many ways! Always be learning.

Your word is a lamp to my feet and a light to my path. Psalms 119:105

REFLECTION TIME

What are some things you need to release in order to find time to rest?

_____

_____

What are some dreams you have for your life (big and small)?

_____

_____

What are some areas where you need to take a RISK?

_____

_____

Set up a daily plan for growing spiritually, physically and emotionally.

_____

_____

If you loved reading this devotional, please leave a review on Amazon. Simply search for the Title of this book and then "write a review". It helps others find it and make the life-changing decision to buy it and read it for themselves. If you enjoy reading Ashley's words, check out her first book on Amazon: Raising A Business & Babies.

THANK YOU

To Bronson: I thank God he brought you into my life eleven years ago! What a life we have created since. We have surpassed my every dream and I am excited for our future. I love you with all my heart! Thanks for believing in my dreams and never telling me I'm crazy!

To Brylee: My one and only daughter. I love you, your heart, your spirit, your mind and your desire to do well in everything you do! I can't wait for our years together to make many beautiful memories!

To Bowen: My heart, my handful. That's what you will always be. You will always be the first little boy who stole my heart and I'll always take delight in seeing you shine!

To Baker: With a strong mind, sweet heart and fierce love, you will be something so special. You already are, my sweet boy. I'll be here supporting you every step of the way.

To Benaiah: My sweetest baby. You are such a light. I love your personality and your smile. You are going to bring us so many laughs and proud moments. I'll be there for your amazing journey, always!

Made in the USA
Monee, IL
27 July 2020

37107445R00039